SECOND EDITION

grade
5

MUSIC THEORY
for Young Musicians

Study Notes with Exercises for ABRSM Theory Exams

Name : ....

Address : ....

Phone : ....

YING YING NG

Published by:

ρoco
STUDIO

Poco Studio Sdn Bhd (646228-V)
B-2-8, IOI Boulevard, Jalan Kenari 5, Bandar Puchong Jaya, 47170 Puchong, Selangor, Malaysia
Tel/Fax: +603 8074 0086   poco_studio@yahoo.co.uk   facebook.com/pocostudio

Copyediting by David C. L. Ngo MA, BAI, PhD, FIET, FBCS, SMIEEE

Printed in Malaysia

ISBN 978-967-10003-5-9

PREFACE

Designed as a workbook to suit the needs of today's young pupils and their teachers, this series presents music theory in a very easy to understand and practical format. Here are some of the pedagogical principles adopted, which make this series unique:

Problem Solving: Breaking a problem into smaller parts makes solving it easier. This series isolates a problem, breaks it into small, manageable parts, and then merges it back into the bigger picture.

Repetition: The key to learning music theory is repetition. Under the lesson plan, the pupil studies component parts incrementally, applying previously acquired skills in the repetitive drills of subsequent lessons.

Association: Children will not learn if repetition is dull. The series creates a fantasy world by using pictures, cartoons and stories to introduce new key words and concepts; this arouses the interest and invokes the imagination of the child, thereby aiding retention of the information.

Challenge: Examinations can provide a challenge to the pupil. This series covers the latest revisions outlined by the Associated Board of the Royal Schools of Music for their theory examinations. It uses effective and efficient drills and exercises that progressively teach the basic concepts. The material is simplified to suit the child's level. The examples and exercises build on language and concepts that children already have, culminating in the acquisition of the skills and knowledge vital to passing the examination.

NOTES ON THE SECOND EDITION

The second edition of Music Theory for Young Musicians brings the practice exercises and examples in the text up to date with the latest ABRSM exam requirements. It also includes many clarifications that update the presentation of the ideas and concepts in the book and thus improve its logical flow. It adds a specimen test in the exam format and provides a set of revision notes on the key areas. All exercises and examples have been revised and many new exercise drills have been added. Concept explanations have been simplified to make it easier to understand. The book's layout has been made clearer by putting the main text against a white background. Additionally, a background colour has been given to each information note to make it more visually inviting.

ACKNOWLEDGE

Cover design and assistance with the illustrations by Amos Tai and the typesetting and layout design by Ivy Chang are gratefully acknowledged. I also extend my sincere thanks to the following persons for advice and suggestions as reviewers of the material:

• Margaret O'Sullivan Farrell BMus, DipMus, LTCL
  Former Course Director, Lecturer in Keyboard Studies
  DIT Conservatory of Music and Drama, Dublin, Ireland
  for her significant contributions to the editing and proofreading of the material.

• Dr. Ita Beausang BMus, MA, PhD, LRAM
  Former Acting Director, Lecturer in Musicianship Studies
  DIT Conservatory of Music and Drama, Dublin, Ireland
  for her many helpful suggestions with regard to the presentation of the material.

Their suggestions for its improvement have helped immeasurably to make it a useful and practical workbook. My grateful thanks also go to my family, David Ngo, Alethia Ngo and Natasha Ngo, for their patience and love that have allowed me to pursue this project.

Ying Ying Ng

CONTENTS

Tenor Clef

- In the **tenor clef**, middle C is on the 4th line.
- The **bassoon**, **cello** and **tenor trombone** all use the tenor clef.

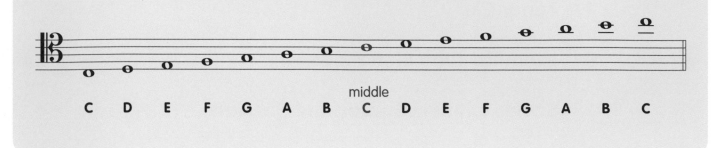

middle

C   D   E   F   G   A   B   C   D   E   F   G   A   B   C

1 **Fill in the missing notes in semibreves** (whole notes)**, and the letter names below the notes.**

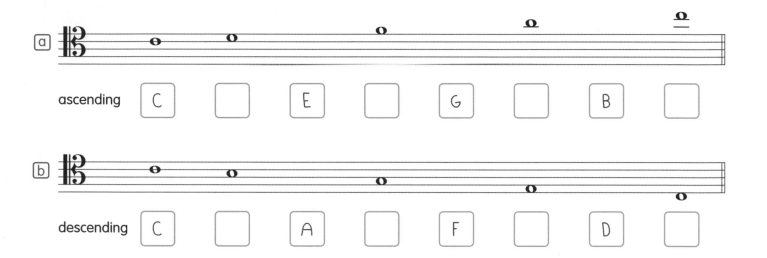

a

ascending   C   [ ]   E   [ ]   G   [ ]   B   [ ]

b

descending   C   [ ]   A   [ ]   F   [ ]   D   [ ]

2 **Write the letter names.**

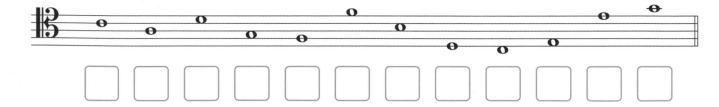

[ ] [ ] [ ] [ ] [ ] [ ] [ ] [ ] [ ] [ ] [ ] [ ]

3 Copy the **tenor clef** and the key signature. Name the major key and minor key for the key signature.

ⓐ

G major

E minor

_____ _____ _____ _____

ⓑ

F major

D minor

_____ _____ _____ _____

4 Write the key signature and **tonic triad** of each key.

ⓐ

A major

ⓑ

Eb major

ⓒ

Ab major

ⓓ

E major

ⓔ

F minor

ⓕ

C# minor

ⓖ

Db major

ⓗ

G# minor

ⓘ

F# minor

ⓙ

Bb major

ⓚ

B major

ⓛ

C minor

5 Write the notes at the same pitch in the treble clef and bass clef.

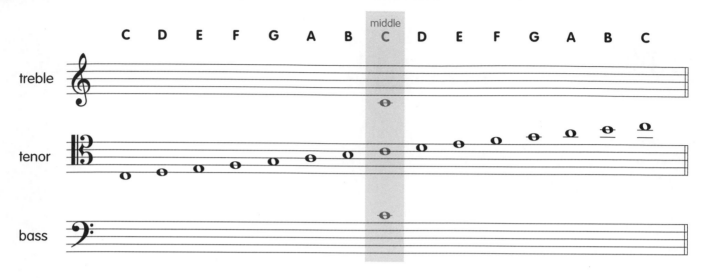

6 Rewrite each note at the same pitch in the tenor clef.

7 Rewrite each tenor clef note at the same pitch in the given clef.

8 **Rewrite each melody at the same pitch in the tenor clef.**

9 Rewrite each melody at the same pitch in the given clef.

Irregular Time Signatures

- In **irregular time**, the number of beats in a bar is not divisible by 2 or 3.
- In $\frac{5}{4}$ and $\frac{5}{8}$, a bar can be grouped as (2+3) or (3+2).
- In $\frac{7}{4}$ and $\frac{7}{8}$, a bar can be grouped as (3+4) or (4+3).

Quintuple time	Septuple time
$\frac{5}{4}$ 5 crotchet beats: 2 + 3	$\frac{7}{4}$ 7 crotchet beats: 3 + 4
$\frac{5}{8}$ 5 quaver beats: 3 + 2	$\frac{7}{8}$ 7 quaver beats: 4 + 3

1 Write the top number for each time signature.

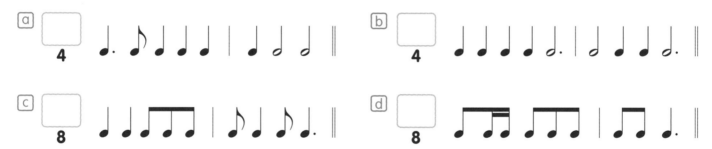

2 Add the correct time signature.

3 Add bar-lines to the rhythm patterns, each of which begins on the 1st beat of the bar.

4 Each extract begins on the 1st beat of the bar, and contains some changes of time signature. Add the correct time signature at the places marked * .

Scales with Six Sharps and Six Flats

F# major and G♭ major

- F# major and G♭ major are **enharmonic equivalents**: they have the same pitch but different letter names.

1 The scales are enharmonic equivalents. **Write the letter names of each scale.**

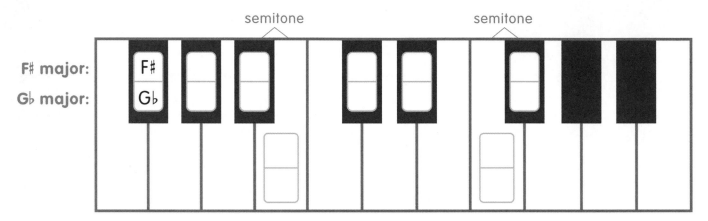

2 **Add any necessary sharps or flats to make each scale. (Do not use a key signature.)**

[a] F# major, ascending

[b] F# major, descending

[c] G♭ major, ascending

[d] G♭ major, descending

3 **Write as semibreves** (whole notes) **each scale, without using a key signature but adding any necessary sharps or flats.**

[a] F# major ascending

[b] G♭ major ascending

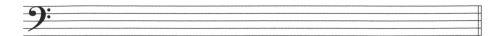

4 **Copy each clef, key signature and key name.**

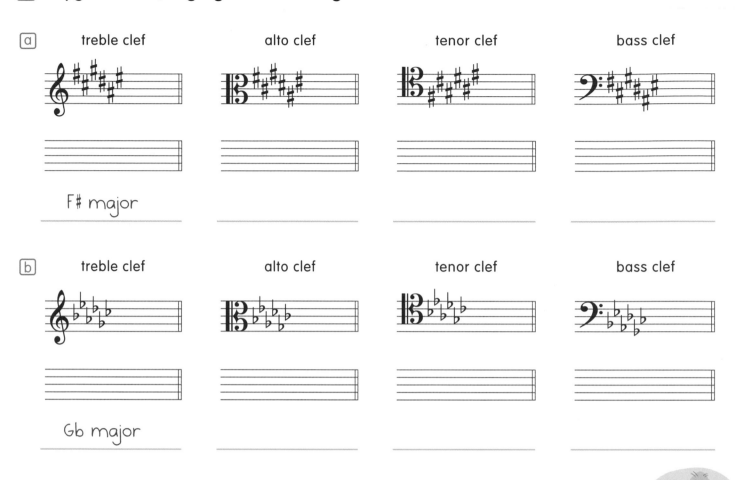

a   treble clef   alto clef   tenor clef   bass clef

F♯ major

b   treble clef   alto clef   tenor clef   bass clef

G♭ major

5 **Write as semibreves** (whole notes) **each scale, using a key signature.**

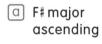

a F♯ major
    ascending

b G♭ major
    descending

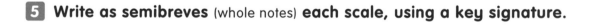

c G♭ major
    ascending

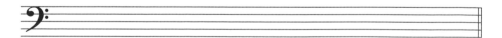

d F♯ major
    descending

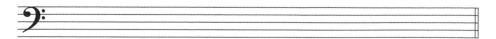

Relative major and minor scales

- The **relative minor** is 3 semitones down from the **relative major**; the relative major is 3 semitones up from the relative minor.

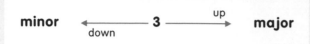

minor ←――― 3 ――↑up――→ major
      down

6 Fill in the relative minors and the key signatures.

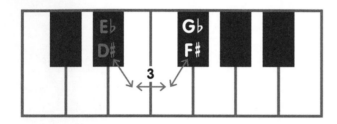

Major	Relative minor	Key signature
F♯ major		F♯,
G♭ major		B♭,

7 Fill in the major and minor keys and their key signatures in the circle of 5ths.

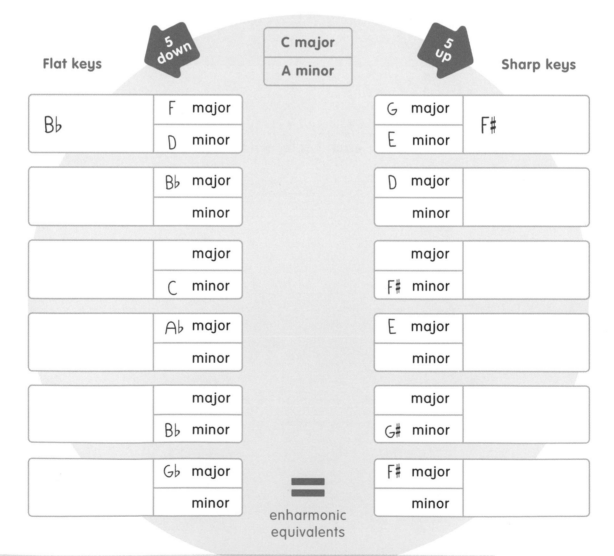

Flat keys   **5 down**   C major / A minor   **5 up**   Sharp keys

| B♭ | F major | | G major | F♯ |
| | D minor | | E minor | |

| | B♭ major | | D major | |
| | minor | | minor | |

| | major | | major | |
| | C minor | | F♯ minor | |

| | A♭ major | | E major | |
| | minor | | minor | |

| | major | | major | |
| | B♭ minor | | G♯ minor | |

| | G♭ major | | F♯ major | |
| | minor | | minor | |

= enharmonic equivalents

Circle of 5ths: p. 32 in **Music Theory for Young Musicians Grade 3**, 2nd Ed.

Harmonic minor

- Raise the **7th note** ascending and descending.

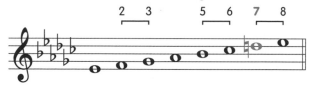

E♭ harmonic minor: B♭ E♭ A♭ D♭ G♭ C♭

With key signature	**Without key signature**

E♭ harmonic minor, ascending

E♭ harmonic minor, ascending

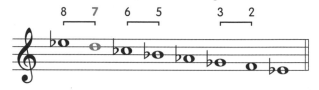

E♭ harmonic minor, descending

E♭ harmonic minor, descending

8 Add the correct clef and key signature to make each harmonic minor scale.
(Raise the 7th note.)

ⓐ D♯ harmonic minor

F♯

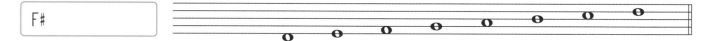

ⓑ E♭ harmonic minor

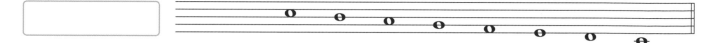

9 Add the correct clef and any necessary sharps or flats to make each harmonic minor scale. (Do not use a key signature but add any necessary accidentals.)

ⓐ D♯ harmonic minor

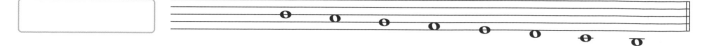

ⓑ E♭ harmonic minor

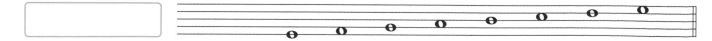

Melodic minor

• Raise the **6th and 7th notes** ascending only.

E♭ melodic minor: B♭ E♭ A♭ D♭ G♭ C♭

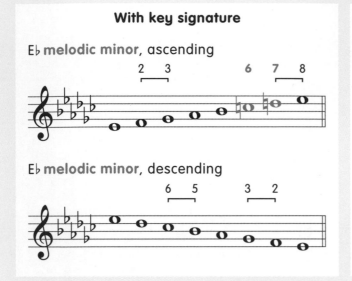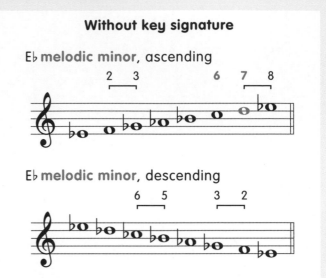

10 Add the correct clef and key signature to make each melodic minor scale.
(Raise the 6th and 7th ascending only.)

ⓐ E♭ melodic minor

ⓑ D♯ melodic minor

11 Add the correct clef and any necessary sharps or flats to make each melodic minor scale. (Do not use a key signature but add any necessary accidentals.)

ⓐ D♯ melodic minor

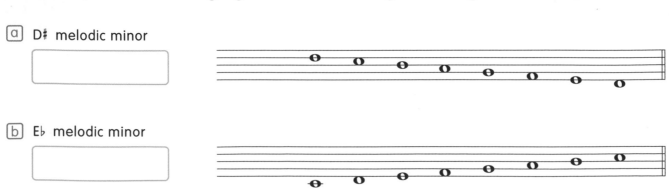

ⓑ E♭ melodic minor

12 **Write as semibreves** (whole notes) **one octave of each scale, beginning on the tonic. (Use a key signature and add any necessary accidentals.)**

a D♯ harmonic minor, ascending

b D♯ melodic minor, descending

c E♭ melodic minor, ascending

d B♭ harmonic minor, ascending

e C♯ melodic minor, descending

f F melodic minor, ascending

g E♭ harmonic minor, ascending

h G♯ harmonic minor, descending

13 **Write as semibreves** (whole notes) **one octave of each scale, beginning on the tonic.**
(Do not use a key signature but add any necessary accidentals.)

[a] D# melodic minor, ascending

[b] E♭ melodic minor, descending

[c] F harmonic minor, descending

[d] G# melodic minor, ascending

[e] D# harmonic minor, descending

[f] B♭ melodic minor, ascending

[g] E♭ harmonic minor, descending

[h] C# harmonic minor, ascending

14 **Write as semibreves** (whole notes) **one octave of each scale, beginning on the given note. (Do not use a key signature but add any necessary accidentals.)**

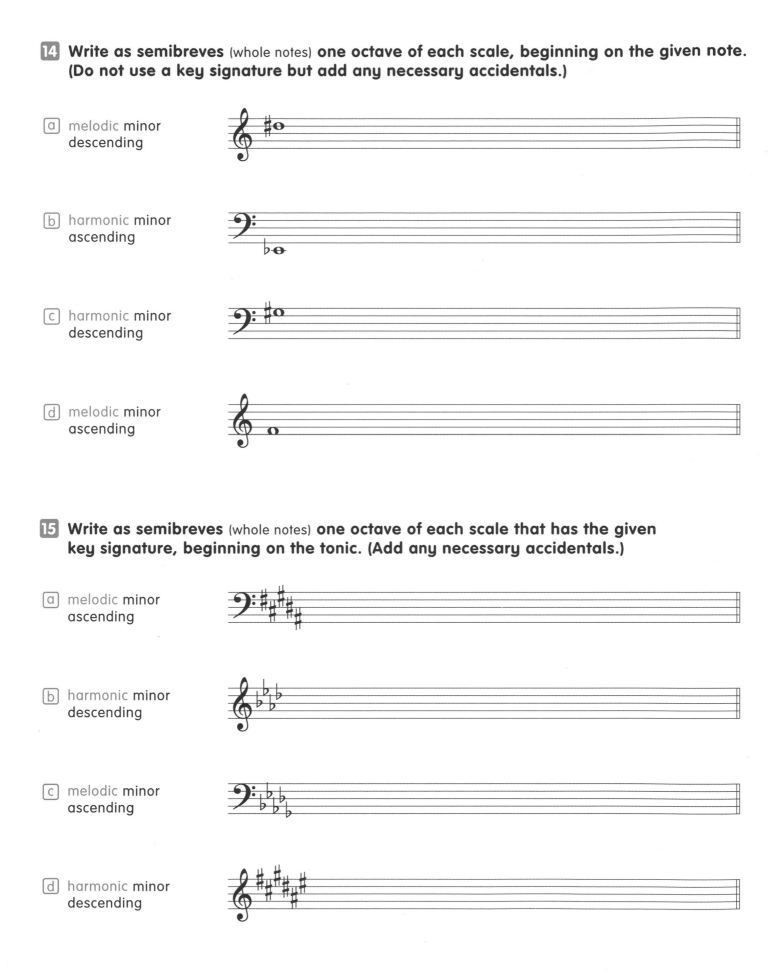

a) melodic minor descending

b) harmonic minor ascending

c) harmonic minor descending

d) melodic minor ascending

15 **Write as semibreves** (whole notes) **one octave of each scale that has the given key signature, beginning on the tonic. (Add any necessary accidentals.)**

a) melodic minor ascending

b) harmonic minor descending

c) melodic minor ascending

d) harmonic minor descending

16 Write as semibreves (whole notes) **one octave ascending of the harmonic minor scale with 6 sharps, beginning on the tonic. (Use a key signature and add any necessary accidentals.)**

17 Write as semibreves (whole notes) **one octave descending of the major scale with 6 flats, beginning on the tonic. (Do not use a key signature but add any necessary accidentals.)**

18 Write the key signature of 5 flats. Using semibreves (whole notes), **write one octave ascending of the melodic minor scale that has the key signature, beginning on the tonic. (Add any necessary accidentals.)**

19 Write the key signature of 4 sharps. Using semibreves (whole notes), **write one octave descending of the major scale that has the key signature, beginning on the tonic.**

- A **chromatic scale** is a scale in semitones that uses all 12 notes (with the 13th note being a repetition of the tonic).

Writing a chromatic scale

❶ Use the tonic and dominant only once.   ❷ Use all other scale degrees twice.
❸ Add the necessary accidentals.

🖊 **Chromatic scale on D, 1 octave ascending**

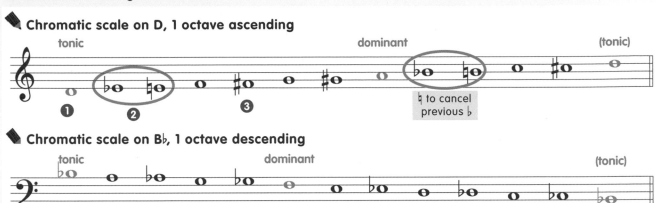

🖊 **Chromatic scale on B♭, 1 octave descending**

> Writing a chromatic scale: p. 44 in **Music Theory for Young Musicians Grade 4**, 2nd Ed.

20 **Write as semibreves** (whole notes) **one octave of the** chromatic **scale, beginning on the given note. (Add any necessary accidentals.)**

[a] ascending

[b] descending

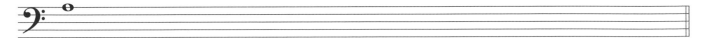

[c] descending

[d] ascending

[e] descending

Transposition

Transposing at the octave

Up 1 octave

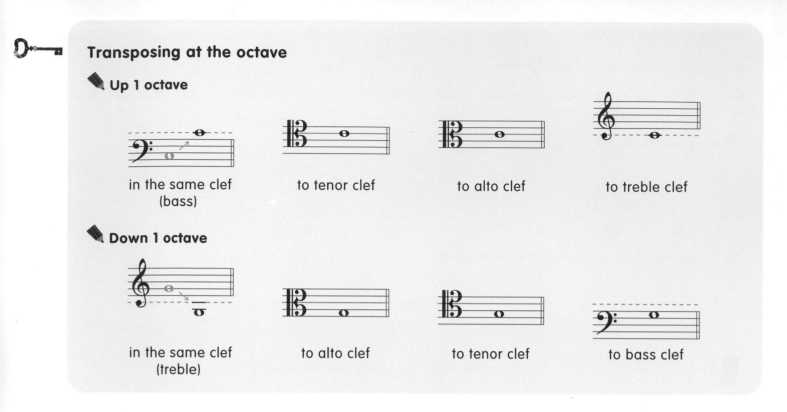

in the same clef (bass)   to tenor clef   to alto clef   to treble clef

Down 1 octave

in the same clef (treble)   to alto clef   to tenor clef   to bass clef

1 Transpose the note up an octave in each given clef.

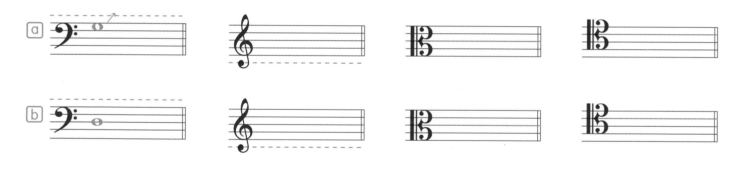

2 Transpose the note down an octave in each given clef.

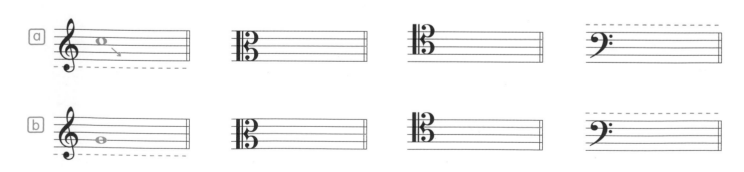

3 Transpose the melody down an octave in each given clef.

4 Transpose the melody up an octave in each given clef.

5 Transpose the melody up an octave in the treble clef, and down an octave in the bass clef.

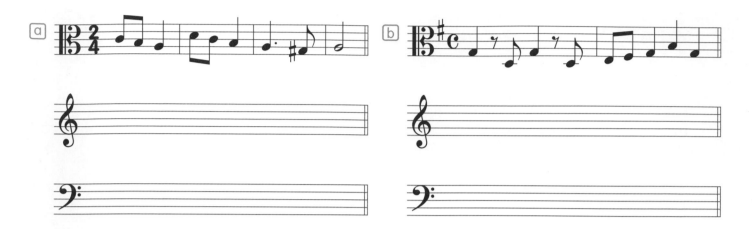

6 Transpose the melody up an octave in the treble clef, and down an octave in the bass clef.

Concert pitch and transposition

- The music for **non-transposing** instruments, such as the piano, is written in **concert pitch**.
  This means that when a piano-player plays a written C, the note that sounds is a C.

- When a player of a **transposing** instrument plays a written C, the note that sounds is NOT a C.
  In the case of a trumpet in B♭, when the player plays a C on the score, the note that sounds is a B♭.

Transposing Instrument	Clarinet in B♭ Trumpet in B♭	Clarinet in A	Horn in F
Written note	(note)	(note)	(note)
Sounding (concert) note	(note) a major 2nd lower	(note) a minor 3rd lower	(note) a perfect 5th lower

Transposing by an interval

Using a key signature

❶ Assume the music is in a **major key**.
❷ Transpose the key signature by the required interval.
❸ Transpose each note by the interval.
❹ Transpose any accidentals by the interval.

Down a major 2nd

Original: G major ❶

Down a perfect 5th

Original: C major

Transposed: F major (B♭) ❷

Transposed: F major (B♭)

Without using a key signature

❶ Assume the music is in a **major key**.
❷ Transpose the key signature by the required interval.
❸ Transpose each note by the interval.
❹ Add all necessary accidentals.

Up a major 2nd

Original: E♭ major ❶

Up a perfect 5th

Original: C major

Transposed: F major (B♭) ❷

Transposed: G major (F♯)

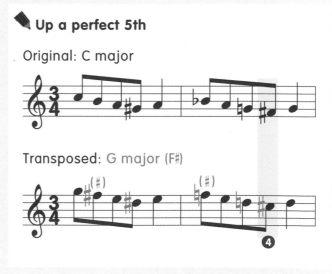

7 **For B♭ instruments, transpose the written key** down a major 2nd **to get the sounding key.**

Written key	C major	F major	G major	D major
Sounding key	B♭ major			

8 **Transpose each melody, which is written for a clarinet in B♭,** down a major 2nd **to get the sounding pitch.**

a **Using a key signature and adding any accidentals**

Mendelssohn

Haydn

b **Without using a key signature but adding any accidentals**

Mozart

Tchaikovsky

9 For B♭ instruments, transpose the sounding key **up a major 2nd** to get the written key.

Written key	D major			
Sounding key	C major	F major	B♭ major	E♭ major

10 Transpose each melody, which is the actual sound made by a trumpet in B♭, **up a major 2nd** to get the written pitch.

[a] Using a key signature and adding any accidentals

Mozart

Mozart

[b] Without using a key signature but adding any accidentals

Tchaikovsky

Haydn

11 For A instruments, transpose the written key down a minor 3rd to get the sounding key.

Written key	C major	F major	B♭ major	E♭ major
Sounding key	A major			

12 Transpose each melody, which is written for a clarinet in A, down a minor 3rd to get the sounding pitch.

a Using a key signature and adding any accidentals

Mozart

Bach

b Without using a key signature but adding any accidentals

Henry Percell

etc.

13 **For A instruments, transpose the sounding key up a minor 3rd to get the written key.**

Written key	Eb major			
Sounding key	C major	D major	G major	A major

14 **Transpose each melody, which is the actual sound made by a clarinet in A, up a minor 3rd to get the written pitch.**

a Using a key signature and adding any accidentals

CPE Bach

Schumann

b Without using a key signature but adding any accidentals

Schubert

etc.

Strauss

15 For F instruments, transpose the written key down a perfect 5th to get the sounding key.

Written key	C major	G major	D major	F major
Sounding Key	F major			

16 Transpose each melody, which is written for a horn in F, down a perfect 5th to get the sounding pitch.

a Using a key signature and adding any accidentals

Telemann

Saint-Saëns

b Without using a key signature but adding any accidentals

Mendelssohn

Tchaikovsky

17 For F instruments, transpose the sounding key up a perfect 5th to get the written key.

Written key	G major			
Sounding key	C major	D major	F major	B♭ major

18 Transpose each melody, which is the actual sound made by a horn in F, up a perfect 5th to get the written pitch.

ⓐ Using a key signature and adding any accidentals

Bach

ⓑ Without using a key signature but adding any accidentals

Bartok

SATB in Short and Open Score

SATB Writing for Voices

- There are usually 4 voice parts in a mixed voice choir: **soprano**, **alto**, **tenor**, and **bass** (SATB).
- Soprano and alto are women's voices; tenor and bass are men's voices.
- Soprano is the highest voice and bass is the lowest.
- Music for SATB is written either on 4 staves (**open score**) or on 2 staves (**short score**).

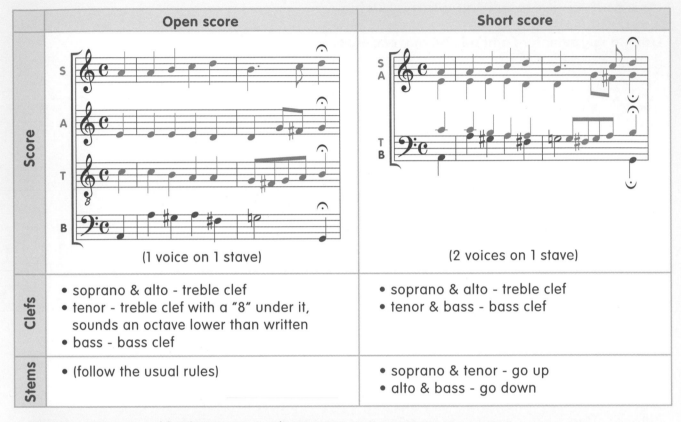

	Open score	Short score
Score	(1 voice on 1 stave)	(2 voices on 1 stave)
Clefs	• soprano & alto - treble clef • tenor - treble clef with a "8" under it, sounds an octave lower than written • bass - bass clef	• soprano & alto - treble clef • tenor & bass - bass clef
Stems	• (follow the usual rules)	• soprano & tenor - go up • alto & bass - go down

- **Mezzo-soprano** and **baritone** are 2 other parts.
- Mezzo-soprano lies between soprano and alto; baritone lies between bass and tenor.
- Highest voice to lowest: **soprano, mezzo-soprano, alto/contralto, tenor, baritone, bass**.

1 **Write out the voices in order.**

a **From lowest to highest**

Alto   Soprano   Mezzo-soprano   Baritone   Bass   Tenor

b **From highest to lowest**

Mezzo-soprano   Contralto   Baritone   Soprano   Tenor   Bass

2 **Rewrite the following in open score.**

C
S
A

Bach

etc.

S

A

etc.

T

B

3 **Rewrite the following in short score.**

L Mason

a
S

A

T

B

S
A

T
B

Irregular time divisions

- A group of 5, 6 or 7 notes uses the same time values as a group of 4 notes.
- A group of 9 notes uses the same time values as a group of 8 notes.

1 **Complete the table.**

Tuplet	Name	Written as 4 or 8 notes	Written as 1 note
	quintuplet		♩
	sextuplet		
	septuplet		
	nontuplet		

2 **Complete each sentence with ♪ , ♩ or 𝅝**

a   is played in the time of a ☐

b   is played in the time of a ☐

c   is played in the time of a ☐

d   is played in the time of a ☐

e   is played in the time of a ☐

f   is played in the time of a ☐

g    is played in the time of a ☐

h   is played in the time of a ☐

i    is played in the time of a ☐

j    is played in the time of a ☐

3 Add the missing bar-lines to the melodies, each of which begins on the 1st beat of the bar.

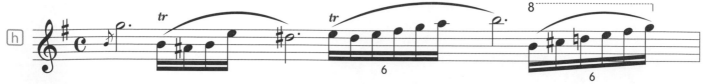

4 Add the time signature to the rhythm patterns, each of which begins on the 1st beat of the bar. Add the correct rest(s) to complete the last bar.

Intervals

- An **interval**, the distance between any 2 notes, has a **number** and a **type**.

Type \ Number	2nd	3rd	4th	5th	6th	7th	8ve
augmented	aug 2nd	aug 3rd	aug 4th	aug 5th	aug 6th	aug 7th	aug 8ve
major/perfect	maj 2nd	maj 3rd	perf 4th	perf 5th	maj 6th	maj 7th	perf 8ve
minor	min 2nd	min 3rd			min 6th	min 7th	
diminished		dim 3rd	dim 4th	dim 5th	dim 6th	dim 7th	dim 8ve

- Intervals larger than 1 octave are **compound intervals**.

major 9th	**major 10th**	**perfect 11th**	**perfect 12th**	**major 13th**	**major 14th**	**perfect 15th**
compound major 2nd	compound major 3rd	compound perfect 4th	compound perfect 5th	compound major 6th	compound major 7th	compound perfect 8ve

Describing a compound interval 🔑

❶ Reduce the compound interval by 1 octave.
❷ Identify the simple interval that results.

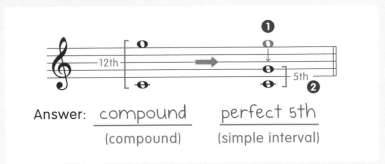

Answer: __compound__   __perfect 5th__
        (compound)   (simple interval)

1 Write a note above the given note to form the harmonic interval.

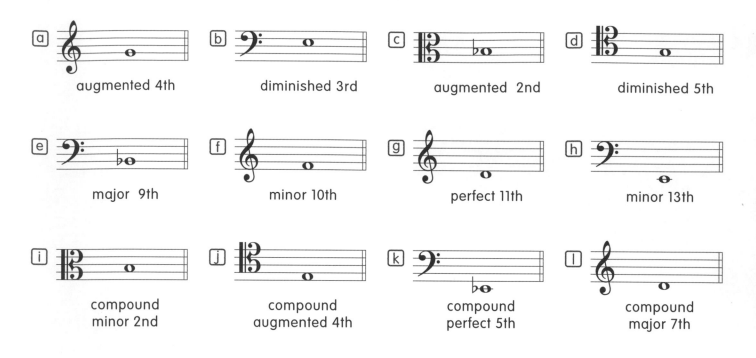

a. augmented 4th

b. diminished 3rd

c. augmented 2nd

d. diminished 5th

e. major 9th

f. minor 10th

g. perfect 11th

h. minor 13th

i. compound minor 2nd

j. compound augmented 4th

k. compound perfect 5th

l. compound major 7th

2 Describe the harmonic interval (e.g. major 2nd).

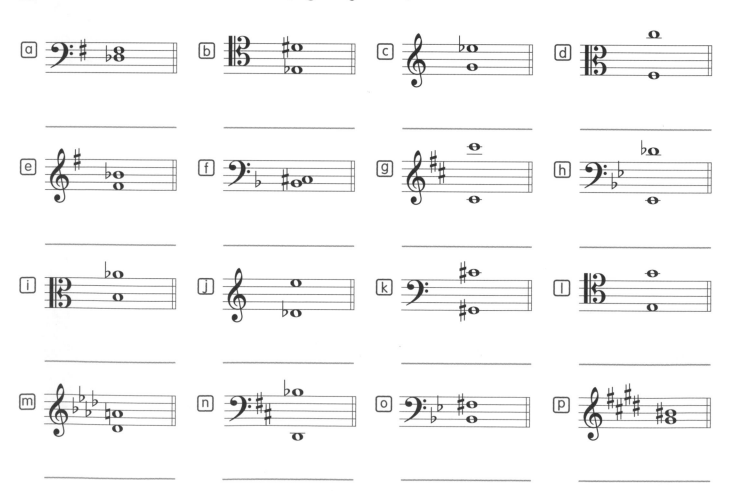

3 **Describe each numbered melodic interval (e.g. major 2nd).**

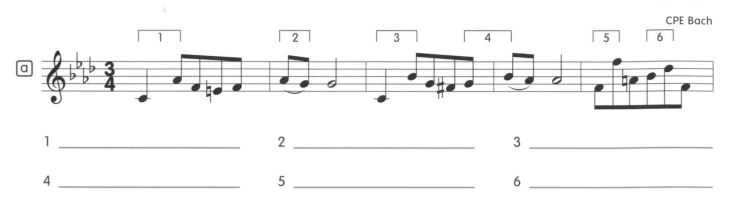

1 _____ 2 _____ 3 _____

4 _____ 5 _____ 6 _____

1 _____ 2 _____ 3 _____

4 _____ 5 _____ 6 _____

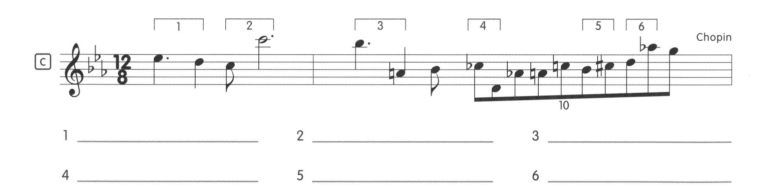

1 _____ 2 _____ 3 _____

4 _____ 5 _____ 6 _____

1 _____ 2 _____ 3 _____

4 _____ 5 _____ 6 _____

4 **Describe each numbered harmonic interval (e.g. major 2nd).**

1 _____ 2 _____ 3 _____

4 _____ 5 _____ 6 _____

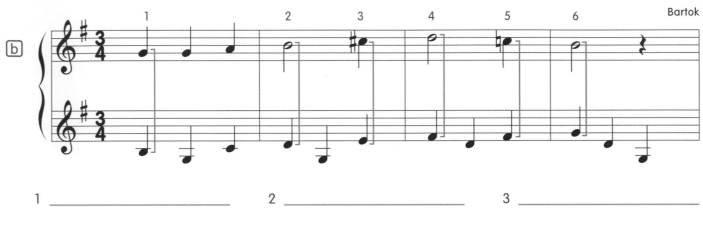

1 _____ 2 _____ 3 _____

4 _____ 5 _____ 6 _____

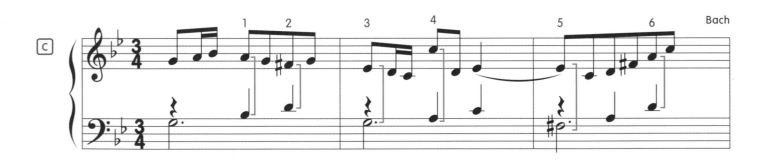

1 _____ 2 _____ 3 _____

4 _____ 5 _____ 6 _____

Identifying Chords

- A **chord** consists of 3 or more notes that sound together; a **triad** is a chord that is built on 3 notes: the root, the 3rd, and the 5th.

- Grade 5 Theory includes the chords formed on tonic (**I**), supertonic (**II**), subdominant (**IV**), and dominant (**V**) in root position (**a** or $\frac{5}{3}$), 1st inversion (**b** or $\frac{6}{3}$) and 2nd inversion (**c** or $\frac{6}{4}$).

1 Circle the letter name for the lowest note of each triad, and write the triad with the given note as the lowest note.

Chord	Root position (root in the bass)	1st inversion (3rd in the bass)	2nd inversion (5th in the bass)
tonic **I**	Ia: (C) E G	Ib: C (E) G	Ic: C E (G)
supertonic **II**	IIa: D F A	IIb: D F A	IIc: D F A
subdominant **IV**	IVa: F A C	IVb: F A C	IVc: F A C
dominant **V**	Va: G B D	Vb: G B D	Vc: G B D

Identifying a chord

❶ Identify the key and write down the triads in the key.
❷ Identify the notes in the given chord.
❸ Identify the triad that has the notes.
❹ Identify the lowest note.

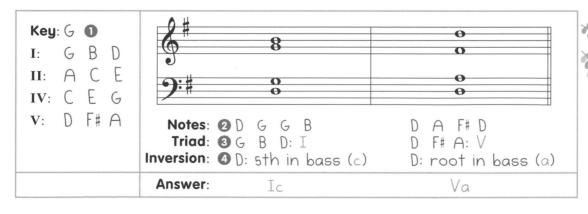

Key: G ❶
I: G B D
II: A C E
IV: C E G
V: D F# A

Notes: ❷ D G G B   D A F# D
Triad: ❸ G B D: I   D F# A: V
Inversion: ❹ D: 5th in bass (c)   D: root in bass (a)

Answer: Ic   Va

2 Fill in the key and its triads. For each chord, identify its notes and then describe it as **Ia, IIb, IVc**, etc.

(a) Key: D major

I : D F# A
II :
IV:
V :

Notes	Ⓓ A D F#				
Chord	Ia				

(b) Key

I :
II :
IV:
V :

Notes					
Chord					

(c) Key

I :
II :
IV:
V :

Notes					
Chord					

(d) Key

I :
II :
IV:
V :

Notes				
Chord				

3 **Fill in the key and its triads. For each numbered chord, identify its notes and then describe it as Ia, IIb, IVc, etc. Circle the 2 successive chords where Ic-V ($\frac{6}{4}$ $\frac{5}{3}$) occurs.**

a

Key

I :

II :

IV:

V :

Notes	1	2	3 DDGB	4 DDF#A	5
Chord			Ic	Va	

b

Key

I :

II :

IV:

V :

5 Schumann

Notes	1	2	3	4	5
Chord					

c

Key

I :

II :

IV:

V :

Handel

Notes	1	2	3	4	5
Chord					

d

Key

I :

II :

IV:

V :

Bach

Notes	1	2	3	4	5
Chord					

Chapter Chords at Cadence Points

- A **cadence** is a 2-chord progression that occurs at the end of a phrase.
- Grade 5 Theory includes only 3 cadences.

Perfect cadence	Plagal cadence	Imperfect cadence
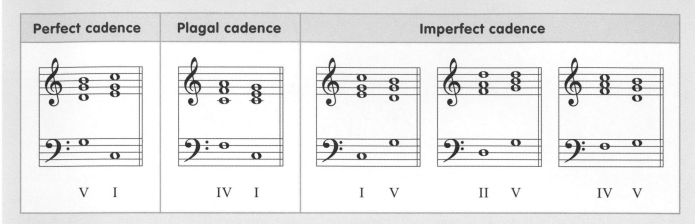		
V I	IV I	I V II V IV V

Identifying a cadence

1. Identify the key and write down the triads in the key.
2. Identify the notes in each chord marked.
3. Identify the possible triads and select the most suitable one.

- For **single notes**, choose 1 of 2 possible triads.

> Each degree of the major scale can be found in 2 of the triads I, II, IV and V, except for the 3rd and the 7th degrees.
>
>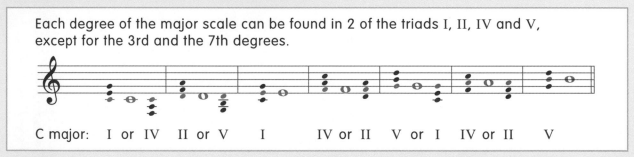
>
> C major: I or IV   II or V   I   IV or II   V or I   IV or II   V

- For **more than 1 note**, choose a triad that contains most of the notes. (Ignore any non-chord notes.)

4. Identify the **cadence**.

✏️ **A chord progression ending with a perfect cadence**

Key: C major ❶		
I: C E G		
II: D F A		
IV: F A C		
V: G B D		

Notes: ❷ D F A   B A G   C C B C
Triad: ❸ II   V   I
Cadence: ❹ perfect cadence

1 Name the key. Indicate 1 chord (I, II, IV or V) at each of the places marked A-E.
(In a 3-chord progression, the last 2 chords define the cadence.)

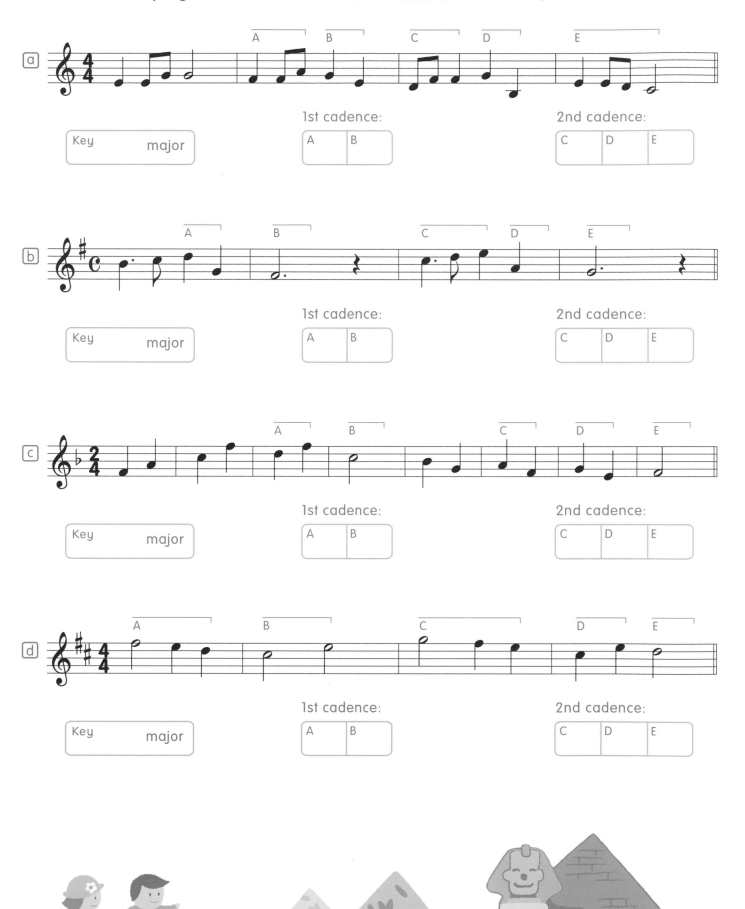

48 | Chords at Cadence Points

Composing Melodies

- An **8-bar melody** is often set out in a **"question-and-answer"** format: it starts off with a 4-bar question, followed by a 4-bar answer.

- The **question** ends with a **dominant chord**, while the **answer** finishes with a **tonic chord**.

1 **Complete the question/answer phrase by choosing the most appropriate 2-bar phrase.**

Composing a melody for an instrument, using a given opening

Setting
❶ Choose: (a) instrument, (b) instrument's range, (c) key, and
(d) form (based on four 2-bar phrases, e.g. **AA¹BC**).

Harmonic structure
❷ Extend the **chord pattern** of the opening, using:
(a) chord **V** at the end of the 2nd phrase,
(b) chord progression **V-I** (**perfect cadence**) at the end of the last phrase, and
(c) chord **I**, **II**, or **IV** for the other bars.

Rhythm & melody
❸ Extend the **melodic and rhythmic pattern** of the opening, making use of
sequence, **imitation** (repetition with variation) and **contrast**.

Performance directions
❹ Add: (a) tempo, (b) dynamics, and (c) articulation (staccato, slur, accents, etc.).

✎ **A melody for violin, in AA¹BC form**

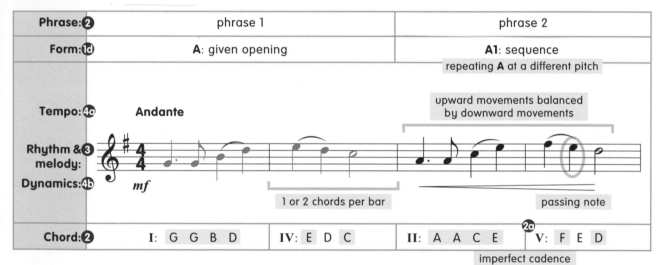

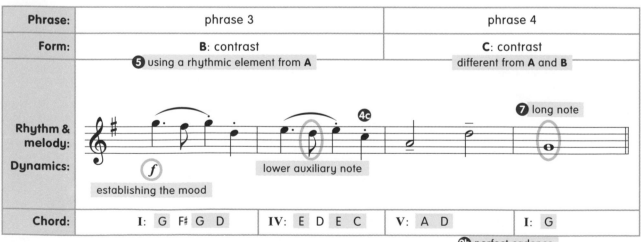

General tips

❺ Re-use ideas from the given opening.

❻ If there is an **upbeat**,
  • make sure the upbeat and last bars add up to 1 complete bar.
  • write phrases that are the same length.

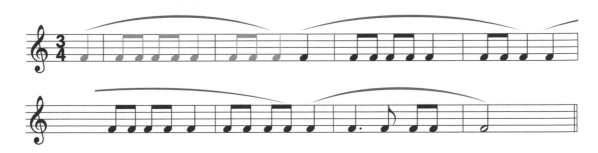

❼ Finish on the tonic chord and with a long note.

❽ Avoid augmented intervals. Avoid large leaps
(such as leaps of a 7th, and leaps greater than 1 octave).

🖋 A melody for flute, in AA¹BC form

Phrase:	phrase 1			phrase 2	
Form:	**A**: given opening			**A1**: sequence ❺ repeating **A** at a different pitch	
Tempo: Rhythm & melody: Dynamics:	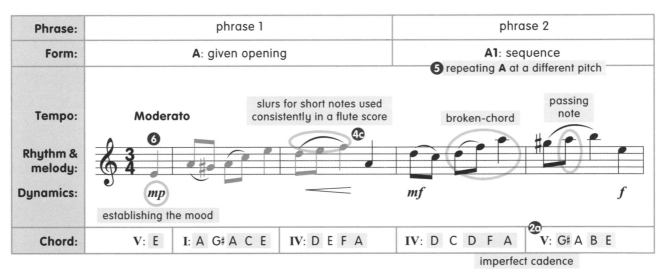				
Chord:	**V**: E	**I**: A G# A C E	**IV**: D E F A	**IV**: D C D F A	**V**: G# A B E

imperfect cadence

Phrase:	phrase 3		phrase 4	
Form:	**B**: contrast using a rhythmic element from **A**		**C**: contrast	
Rhythm & melody: Dynamics:	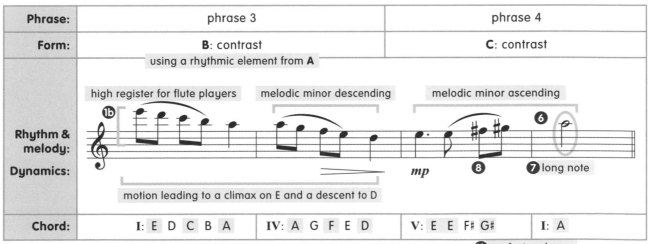			
Chord:	**I**: E D C B A	**IV**: A G F E D	**V**: E E F# G#	**I**: A

❷ᵇ perfect cadence

1 Motifs using chord notes

C major

I: G E C E   V: D B G

A minor

V: E G♯ B   I: C A

---

2 Name the key. Using the given rhythm, compose a 2-bar melody using notes from the given chord sequence.

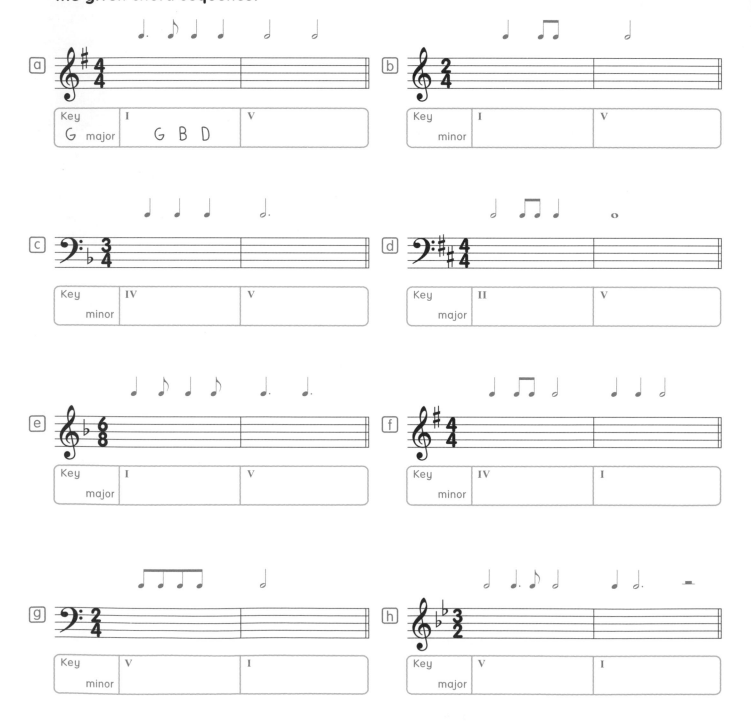

a

Key	I	V
G major	G B D	

b

Key	I	V
minor		

c

Key	IV	V
minor		

d

Key	II	V
major		

e

Key	I	V
major		

f

Key	IV	I
minor		

g

Key	V	I
minor		

h

Key	V	I
major		

2 Motifs using chord notes and non-chord notes

- A **passing note** P is a non-chord note which moves stepwise between 2 chord notes a 3rd apart.
- An **auxiliary note** A is a non-chord note which moves stepwise between 2 repeated chord notes.

C major

I: G A G C E   V: D C B A G

A minor

V: B E F# G#   I: A G# A

3 Name the key. Compose a 2-bar melody by using chord notes and adding non-chord notes.

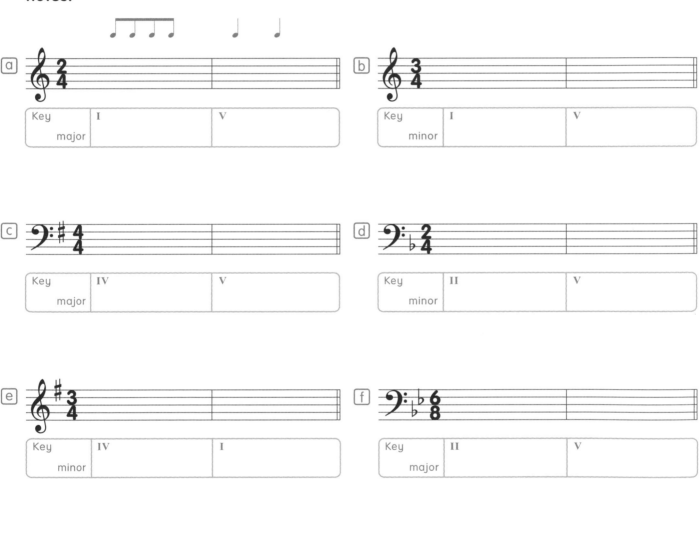

Motifs based on sequence, repetition or inversion

- **Sequence:** A motif repeated at a different pitch

- **Imitation** (repetition with variation): A motif repeated with a slight change

- **Inversion:** A motif repeated upside down

4 **Name the key. Write a melody with the given opening motif using:**

[a] **Sequence**

(i)

Key: _____

(ii)

Key: _____

(iii)

Key: _____

(use melodic minor scale)

(iv)

Key: _____

b **Imitation**

(i)

Key: _____

I

(ii)

Key: _____

I

c **Inversion**

(i)

Key: _____

I

(ii)

Key: _____

I

Composing Melodies | **55**

5 Name the key. Compose a melody, using the given opening. (End the 1st half with an imperfect cadence, and the 2nd half with a perfect cadence.)

ⓐ Key: _____

ⓑ Key: _____

ⓒ Key: _____

ⓓ Key: _____

6 Compose a melody, using the given opening. (Add tempo, dynamics and articulation.)

a **For violin, flute or trumpet**

(i) Key: _____ Instrument _____

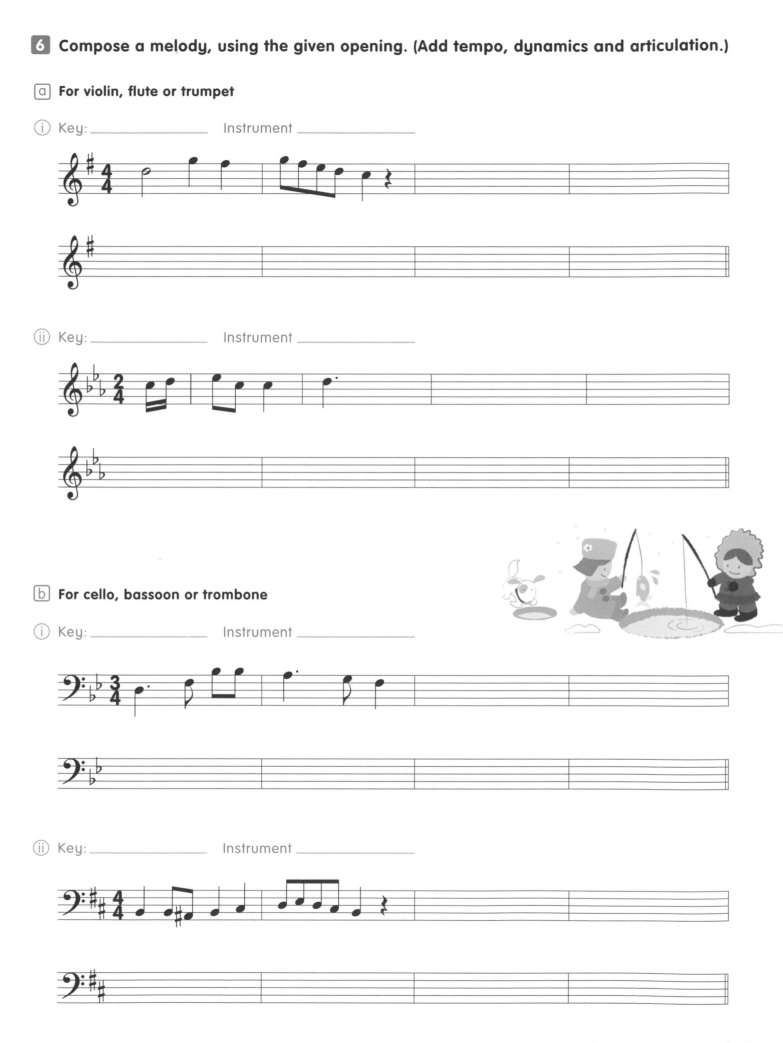

(ii) Key: _____ Instrument _____

b **For cello, bassoon or trombone**

(i) Key: _____ Instrument _____

(ii) Key: _____ Instrument _____

Composing a Melody to Given Words

❶ Find out which words or syllables are strong.
   (a) Say the words a few times, to see where the natural **stresses** fall.
   (b) Write out the words, dividing words of more than one syllable by using a **hyphen**:

   wa–ter, beau–ti–ful, ex–plan–a–tion

   (c) Mark the stressed (strong) syllables.

   Hump-ty Dump-ty sat on a wall

   Hump-ty Dump-ty had a great fall.

   (d) There may be a "**silent stress**" where you feel the need to pause.
       Hold the note, with a **tie** if necessary, or use a **rest**.

   Hick-o-ry, dick-o-ry, dock (–)

   The mouse ran up the clock (–)

❷ Choose a time signature.
   (a) Decide if the smallest value will be a quaver or a crotchet.
   (b) Decide if there will be 1 stress/bar (usually in $\frac{2}{4}$ and $\frac{3}{4}$) or 2 stresses/bar (usually $\frac{4}{4}$ and $\frac{6}{8}$).
   (c) Put in bar-lines.

   • 1 stress/bar: Put a bar-line before every stress.

   My | dar – ling | start – ed to | leave | me

   To | sail on the | deep blue | sea. | (–) ‖

   • 2 stresses/bar: Put a bar-line before the 1st stress, and then before every 2nd stress.

   My | dar – ling   start – ed to | leave me

   To | sail on the deep blue | sea. (–) ‖

❸ Write the rhythm:

   • First, above the words:

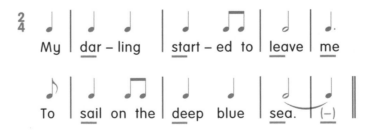

   • Then, as a continual pattern:

- For variety and interest, 2 equal notes or 3 equal notes may be changed rhythmically:

4 Decide on the **key** and **voice range**, as well as a **tempo** to suit the **mood of the words**.

5 Compose a melody for the words, keeping in mind that it is for vocal performance.
(a) Each syllable will normally get one note.
(b) If there are 2 or more notes for a single syllable, **slur** the notes to show this.

6 Put in markings for **tempo** and **dynamics**, and if you like, some staccato **articulations**.

✎ **1 stress per bar in 2/4 and 3/4**

✎ **2 stresses per bar in 4/4 and 6/8**

7 Find out which words/syllables are strong and underline them.
Choose a time signature and put a bar-line before every strong word/syllable.
Write at least one note for each syllable.

[a]   <u>Be</u>autiful | <u>drea</u>mer, queen of my song,

$\frac{3}{4}$ ♩ ♩ ♩ | | | ‖

Beau - ti - ful

[b]   The friendly cow, all red and white, I love with all my heart:

8 Find out which words/syllables are strong and underline them.
Choose a time signature and put a bar-line before every strong word/syllable.
Write the rhythm and compose a melody for the words.

<u>Christ</u>mas is | <u>co</u>ming! The | <u>goose</u> is getting | <u>fat</u>;
Please to put a pen ny in the old man's hat,

$\frac{2}{4}$ ♩ ♫ | ♪ ♩ ♪ | | |

Christ-mas is   co - ming! The goose is get - ting   fat,

9 **Compose a melody for voice to the given words. (Write at least one note per syllable. Add performance directions as appropriate.)**

[a]
First I saw the white bear, then I saw the black;
Then I saw the camel with a hump upon his back;

William Makepeace Thackeray

[b]
Dance, little baby, dance up high,
Never mind baby, mother is by;

Ann Taylor

[c]
The day is past, the sun is set,
And the white stars are in the sky;

Thomas Miller

Ornaments and Repetitions

- An **ornament** decorates a note by adding extra notes.
- **Baroque** music is decorated with ornaments.

Name	Symbol	Written		Played	
appoggiatura, leaning note	♪	ⓐ	ⓑ	ⓐ	ⓑ
acciaccatura, crushed/grace note	♪				
acciaccature crushed/grace notes	♫				
turn	∼	ⓐ	ⓑ	ⓐ	ⓑ (3)
inverted turn	∽				
upper mordent	⌁	ⓐ	ⓑ	ⓐ	ⓑ
lower mordent	⌁	ⓐ	ⓑ	ⓐ	ⓑ
trill, shake	*tr*	*tr*	*tr* or		(3)
arpeggiation, spread sign	}				

• Among the standard methods of simplifying music notation are:

Repetition	Written	Played
repeated quavers	ⓐ ⓑ	ⓐ ⓑ
repeated semiquavers	ⓐ ⓑ ⓐ ⓑ	ⓐ ⓑ ⓐ ⓑ
repeated chords/quaver groups	ⓐ ⓑ	ⓐ ⓑ
repeated semiquaver groups		
repeated groups of mixed notes		
repeated bars		
multiple bar rests (number = number of bar rests)	3	

1 Name each ornament.

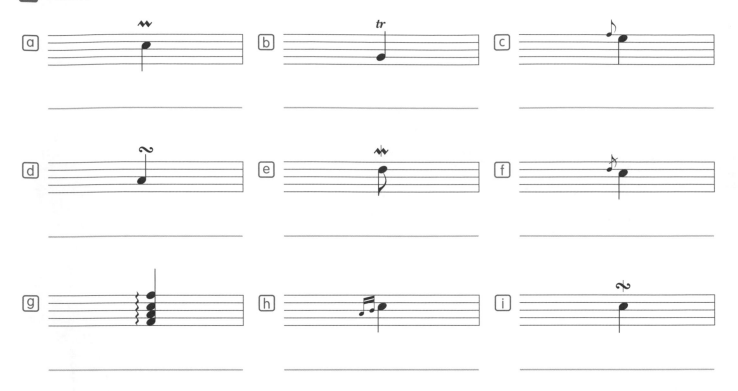

a

b

c

d

e

f

g

h

i

2 Mark each ornament with the appropriate letter.

A an upper turn   **B** an appoggiatural   **C** a lower mordent

D an upper mordent   **E** a trill   **F** an acciaccatura

3 Name each written-out ornament.

_____   _____

_____   _____

_____   _____

4 Mark each ornament/repetition with the appropriate letter, and give the bar in which it occurs.

A an acciaccatura.   Bar _____

B an arpeggiation.   Bar _____

C 3 bar rests.   Bar _____

D a repeated bar.   Bar _____

E repeated semiquavers in the time of one crotchet. Bar _____

Instruments

The 4 families in the orchestra are: **strings**, **woodwind**, **brass** and **percussion**.

String family instrument
- has 4 strings.
- makes sound by one hand drawing a **bow** across the **strings,** or plucking them, and the fingers of the other hand change the notes.
- can produce more than 1 note at a time.
- can be played with a mute (**con sordino**).

highest-sounding ←————————————→ lowest-sounding

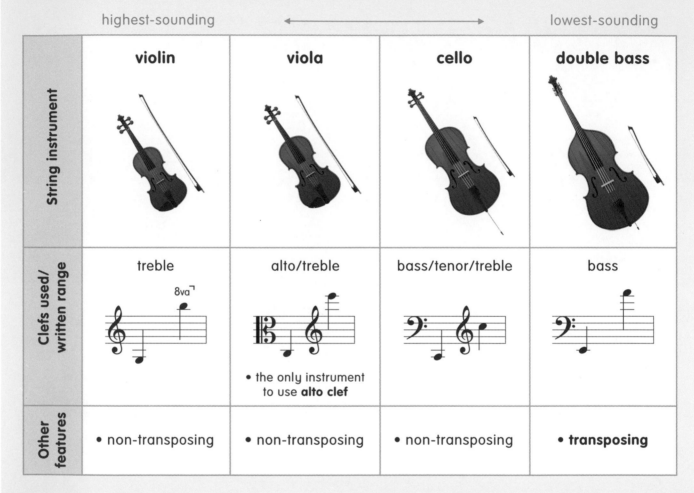

String instrument	violin	viola	cello	double bass
Clefs used/ written range	treble	alto/treble	bass/tenor/treble	bass
		• the only instrument to use **alto clef**		
Other features	• non-transposing	• non-transposing	• non-transposing	• **transposing**

Performance directions

arco	: play with the bow	⌢♩♩♩♩	: play in one bow stroke
con sordini	: with mutes		
senza sordini	: without mutes	⊓	: down bow
pizzicato, pizz.	: pluck the strings	V	: up bow
sul G	: play on the G string		: double stop
sul ponticello	: play near the bridge		(play two strings at once)

1 **Answer the questions about the string family.**

a Name the string instruments with the most usual clef for each in order from highest to lowest.

Instrument	Violin			
Clef	treble			

b Name 1 instrument that is sometimes played using **pizzicato** and state the family to which it belongs.

Instrument _____ Family _____ .

c The **violin** belongs to the _____ family. The **lowest-sounding** member of that family is the

_____ and it normally uses the _____ clef.

d The instrument next in pitch above the **cello** is the _____ and it normally uses the

_____ clef.

e The only **transposing** string instrument is the _____

f The only instrument that uses the **alto clef** is the _____

g Give the meaning of:

ⓘ arco _____   ⓘⓘ senza sordini _____

ⓘⓘⓘ sul G _____   ⓘⓥ sul ponticello _____

ⓥ pizzicato _____   ⓥⓘ con sordini _____

Woodwind family instrument

- is a tube of wood or metal.
- makes sound by blowing air through a **reed** or across a **mouthpiece**, notes are changed by covering and uncovering holes with fingers or **keys**.
- can only produce 1 note at a time.

highest-sounding ⟵⟶ lowest-sounding

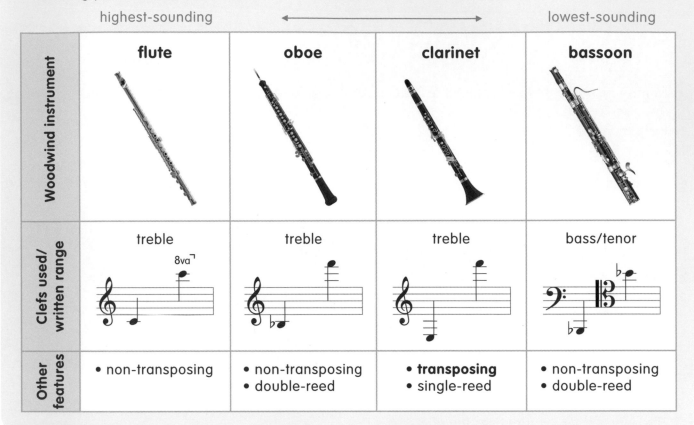

	flute	oboe	clarinet	bassoon
Clefs used/ written range	treble	treble	treble	bass/tenor
Other features	• non-transposing	• non-transposing • double-reed	• **transposing** • single-reed	• non-transposing • double-reed

---

2 **Answer the questions about the woodwind family.**

a Name the woodwind instruments with the most usual clef for each in order from highest to lowest.

Instrument				
Clef				

b Name 1 **single-reed** instrument and 2 **double-reed** instruments.

Single-reed _____ Double-reed _____ _____

c Name 1 **transposing** woodwind instrument. _____

d Name 1 woodwind instrument that could play at the same pitch as the **cello**. _____

e Name 2 woodwind instruments that could play music written in the **treble clef**.

_____ _____

f The **oboe** belongs to the _____ family and the **lowest-sounding** member of that family

is the _____ .

Brass family instrument
- is a long, coiled tube of metal.
- makes sound by buzzing with the lips while blowing in a **mouthpiece**, and notes are changed by **valves** or a **slide**.
- can only produce 1 note at a time.
- can be played with a mute (**con sordino**).

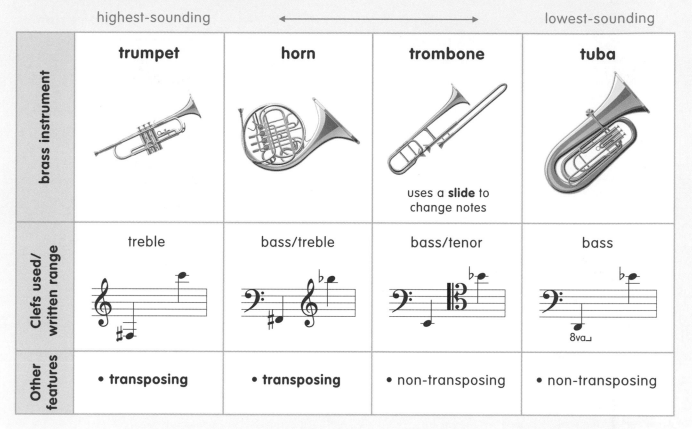

highest-sounding ⟷ lowest-sounding

brass instrument	trumpet	horn	trombone	tuba
			uses a **slide** to change notes	
Clefs used/ written range	treble	bass/treble	bass/tenor	bass
Other features	• **transposing**	• **transposing**	• non-transposing	• non-transposing

---

3 **Answer the questions about the brass family.**

[a] Name the brass instruments with the most usual clef for each in order from highest to lowest.

Instrument				
Clef				

[b] Name 1 brass instrument that uses a **slide**. _____

[c] The **lowest-sounding** brass instrument is the _____ and it normally uses

_____ clef.

[d] Name 2 **transposing** brass instruments. _____   _____

Percussion family instrument

- is made of skin, wood or metal.
- produces sound when the instrument is struck or shaken.
- makes a definite pitch or indefinite pitch.

Definite pitch	Clef	Indefinite pitch
timpani (kettle drums) • the only drums that can produce notes in definite pitch	bass	**side drum**
glockenspiel • has metal bars	treble	**bass drum**
xylophone • has wooden bars	treble	**cymbals**
marimba • has wooden bars with resonators	treble & bass	**triangle**
vibraphone • has metal bars with resonators	treble	**tambourine**
celesta • has metal bars with a keyboard	treble & bass	**castanets**
tubular bells	treble	**tam-tam (gong)**

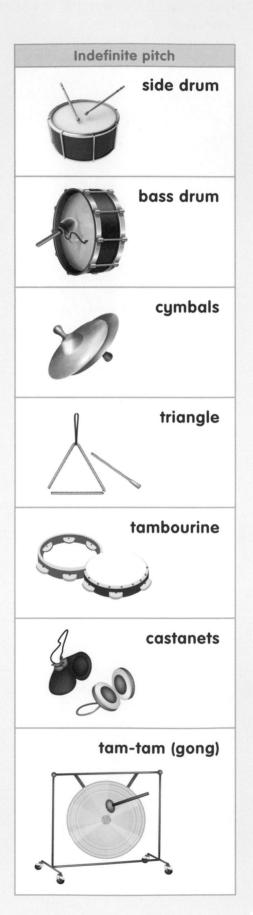

Stringed keyboard instrument
- played using a keyboard.
- produces sound through the vibration of strings.
- can produce more than 1 note at a time.

piano
- has a keyboard with 88 keys.
- produces sound by pressing a **key** that activates a **hammer** to **strike** the string.

treble

bass

Performance directions	
mano destra, m.d.	: right hand
mano sinistra, m.s.	: left hand
con pedale	: with pedal
senza pedale	: without pedal
una corda (1 string)	: press the left pedal
tre corde (3 strings)	: release the left pedal
𝄻. ✻ or P ⌐___⌐	: press or release the right pedal
{	: spread the notes of the chord quickly, starting from the bottom

clavichord
- produces sound by pressing a **key** that activates a blade (called a **tangent**) to **strike** the string.
- produces softer sound than the piano.
- smaller than the piano.

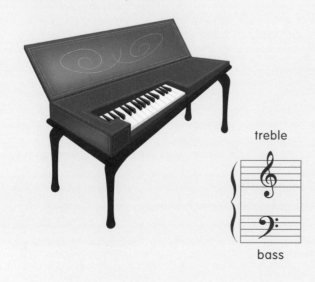

treble

bass

harpsichord
- produces sound by pressing a **key** that activates a **jack** with a **plectrum** on it; this plectrum **plucks** the string.

treble

bass

4 **Answer the questions about the percussion family.**

a Name 4 percussion instruments, 2 with **indefinite pitch** and 2 with **definite pitch**.

Indefinite pitch _____   _____

Definite pitch _____   _____

b The only **drums** with definite pitch are the _____ . They are also called

_____ . They use the _____ clef.

c Underline 1 percussion instrument that produces sounds of **indefinite pitch**.

     timpani   marimba   tambourine   glockenspiel

d The _____ is a keyboard instrument whose strings are **plucked** and the

_____ is a keyboard instrument whose strings are **struck**.

e Name 2 keyboard instruments other than the **piano**.

_____   _____

f Give the meaning of:

(i) una corda : _____   (ii) mano sinistra : _____

(iii) tre corde : _____   (iv) mano destra : _____

5 **Answer the questions about the the 4 families of the orchestra.**

a Name the **lowest-sounding** member and the **highest-sounding** member of each family.

Family	Lowest -sounding	Highest-sounding
string		
woodwind		
brass		

b   Underline 1 instrument that could play at the same pitch as the **violin**.

       double bass   flute   tuba   timpani

       State the family to which it belongs. _____

c   Give 1 reason why no **brass** or **woodwind** instrument could play the following.

       Reason _____

       _____

d   Underline 2 families of instruments that are often played **con sordini**.

       string   woodwind   brass

e   State the family to which each instrument belongs.

       bassoon   tambourine   cello   trombone

       String _____   Woodwind _____

       Percussion _____   Brass _____

f   The **clarinet** is a member of the _____ family.

g   No **brass** or **woodwind** instrument could play more than one note at a time. _____ (TRUE / FALSE).

h   Name 3 instruments, 1 **string**, 1 **woodwind** and 1 **brass**, which use each clef.

       Tenor clef : String _____ Woodwind _____ Brass _____

       Bass clef : String _____ Woodwind _____ Brass _____

i   Name 1 **woodwind** or **brass** instrument that could play a piece of **cello** music so that it sounds at the same pitch, and state the family to which it belongs.

       Instrument _____ Family _____

j. Name 1 instrument of each family that could play the following, and state whether it is a **transposing** or **non-transposing** instrument.

Family	Instrument	Transposing/Non-transposing
string		
woodwind		
brass		

k. Name 1 instrument of each family that could play the following:

String _____ Woodwind _____ Brass _____

l. Complete the table to show which clef(s) each instrument uses.

Family	Instrument	Treble clef	Alto clef	Tenor clef	Bass clef
string	violin	✓			
	viola				
	cello				
	double bass				
woodwind	flute				
	oboe				
	clarinet				
	bassoon				
brass	trumpet				
	horn				
	trombone				
	tuba				

Performance Directions

Italian terms

a	at, to, by, for, in the style of	**da capo, D.C.**	repeat from the beginning
accelerando, accel.	gradually getting faster	**dal segno, D.S.**	repeat from the sign 𝄋
ad libitum, ad lib.	at choice, freely	**deciso**	with determination
adagietto	rather slow (faster than **adagio**)	**decrescendo, decresc.**	gradually getting softer
adagio	slow	**delicato**	delicate
affettuoso	tenderly	**diminuendo, dim.**	gradually getting softer
affrettando	hurrying	**dolce**	sweet, soft
agitato	agitated	**dolente**	sad, mournful
al, alla	to the, in the manner of (**alla breve**: with a minim beat, 𝄵 (2/2); **alla marcia**: in the style of a march)	**dolore**	grief (**doloroso**: sorrowful)
		doppio movimento	twice as fast
		e, ed	and
		energico	energetic
allargando	broadening (getting slower and louder)	**espressivo, express., espr.**	expressive (**espressione**: expression; **con espressione**: with expression)
allegretto	fairly fast (slower than **allegro**)		
allegro	fast (**allegro assai**: very fast)	**estinto**	as soft as possible, lifeless
amabile	amiable, pleasant	*f*, **forte**	loud
amore	love (**amoroso**: loving)	**facile**	easy
andante	at a medium (walking) speed	*ff*, **fortissimo**	very loud
andantino	slightly faster than **andante**	**fine**	the end
anima	soul, spirit (**con anima**: with feeling)	**forza**	force
		fp, **fortepiano**	loud, then immediately soft
animando	becoming lively	**fuoco**	fire
animato	animated, lively	**giocoso**	playful, merry
appassionato	with passion	**giusto**	proper, exact (**tempo giusto**: in strict time)
assai	very		
attacca	go straight on	**grave**	very slow, solemn
ben	well	**grazioso**	graceful
brio	vigour (**con brio**: with vigour)	**incalzando**	getting faster
calando	getting softer, dying away	**l'istesso**	the same (**l'istesso tempo**: at the same speed)
cantabile	in a singing style		
cantando	singing	**lacrimoso**	sad
come	as, similar to (**come prima**: as before; **come sopra**: as above)	**largamente**	broadly
		larghetto	rather slow (faster than **largo**)
		largo	slow, stately
comodo	convenient, comfortable (**tempo comodo**: at a comfortable (normal) speed)	**legato**	smoothly
		leggiero	light, nimble
		lento	slow
con, col	with	**loco**	at the normal pitch (used to cancel 8va)
crescendo, cresc.	gradually getting louder		

Newly introduced terms for grade 5 are highlighted in colour.

Italian terms (Cont.)

lunga	long (**lunga pausa**: long pause)	rinforzando, rf, rfz	reinforcing
		risoluto	bold, strong
lusingando	coaxing, in a sweet and persuasive style	ritardando, ritard., rit.	gradually getting slower
ma	but	ritenuto, riten., rit.	held back
maestoso	majestic	ritmico	rhythmically
marcato, marc.	emphatic, accented	rubato, tempo rubato	with some freedom of time
marziale	in a military style		
meno	less	scherzando, scherzoso	playful, joking
mesto	sad		
mezzo	half	seconda, secondo	second
mf, mezzo forte	moderately loud	segue	go straight on
misura	measure (**alla misura**: in strict time; **senza misura**: in free time)	semplice	simple, plain
		sempre	always
		senza	without
moderato	moderately	sforzando, sforzato, sf, sfz	forced, accented
molto	very, much		
morendo	dying away	simile, sim.	in the same way
mosso, moto	movement (**meno mosso**: slower; **con moto**: with movement)	smorzando, smorz.	dying away
		sonoro	resonant, with rich tone
		sopra	above
mp, mezzo piano	moderately soft	sostenuto	sustained
niente	nothing (**a niente**: dying away)	sotto	below (**sotto voce**: in an undertone)
nobilmente	nobly		
non	not	staccato, stacc.	detached
ossia	or, alternatively	stringendo	gradually getting faster
p, piano	soft	subito	suddenly
perdendosi	dying away	tanto	so much
pesante	heavy	tempo	speed, time (**a tempo**: in time)
piacevole	pleasant	teneramente, tenerezza	tenderly, tenderness
piangevole	plaintive, in the style of a lament		
		tenuto	held
più	more	tosto	swift, rapid
pochettino, poch.	rather little	tranquillo	calm
poco	a little	triste, tristamente	sad, sorrowful
possibile	possible (**presto possibile**: as fast as possible)	troppo	too much
		veloce	swift
pp, pianissimo	very soft	vivace, vivo	lively, fast
presto	fast (faster than **allegro**)	voce	voice
prima, primo	first	volante	flying, fast
quasi	as if, resembling	volta	time (**prima volta**: 1st time; **seconda volta**: 2nd time)
rallentando, rall.	gradually getting slower		

French terms

à	to, at
animé	animated, lively
assez	enough, sufficiently
avec	with
cédez	yield, slow down
douce	sweet
en dehors	prominent
et	and
léger, légère	light
légèrement	light
lent	slow
mais	but
moins	less
modéré	at a moderate speed
non	not
peu	little
plus	more
presser	hurry (**en pressant**: hurrying on)
ralentir	slow down
retenu	held back (**en retenant**: holding back, slowing a little)
sans	without
très	very
un / une	one
vif	lively
vite	fast

German terms

aber	but
Ausdruck	expression
bewegt	with movement, agitated
breit	broad, expansive
ein	a, one
einfach	simple
etwas	somewhat, rather
fröhlich	cheerful, joyful
immer	always
langsam	slow
lebhaft	lively
mässig	at a moderate speed
mit	with
nicht	not
ohne	without
ruhig	peaceful
schnell	fast
sehr	very
süss	sweet
traurig	sad
und	and
voll	full
wenig	little
wieder	again
zart	tender, delicate
zu	to, too

Music signs

♩	♩	hold, pause
♩	♩	slight pressure
♩	♩	accent
♩	♩	strong accent
♩♩♩		**semi-staccato:** slightly detached, non legato
♩	♩	**staccato**: detached, short
♩	♩	**staccatissimo:** very detached, very short
♩.	♩.	**dot**: play the note longer by half its value
♩♩		**tie**: play the 1st note and hold it for the time of both notes
♩♩		**slur**: play the notes smoothly

(crescendo)	gradually getting louder
(diminuendo)	gradually getting softer
8va	octave
8va / 8	play an octave higher
8va / 8	play an octave lower
and	**repeat marks**: repeat between marks
M.M. ♩ = 96 or ♩ = 96	96 crotchet beats in a minute

1 **Give the meaning of:**

a langsam _____

b schnell _____

c risoluto _____

d molto tranquillo _____

e allegro vivace _____

f mezzo voce _____

g perdendosi _____

h adagio, ma non troppo _____

i tre corde _____

j molto giocoso _____

k ad lib. _____

l maestoso _____

m très modéré _____

n allegro assai _____

o ben legato _____

p affettuoso _____

q molto cantabile _____

r traurig _____

s smorzando _____

t andante con espressione _____

u adagio sostenuto ed espressivo _____

2 **Underline the 2 words that are similar in meaning to each given word.**

a **allegro** : lent vite schnell

b **dolce** : süss douce animé

c **largo** : lent peu langsam

d **mesto** : lacrimoso traurig mässig

e **vivace** : douce vite schnell

f **dolente** : traurig lacrimoso ruhig

g **con** : avec non mit

h **ma** : aber mais nicht

Grade 5 Specimen Test

TOTAL MARKS
100

Duration: 2 hours

1 Look at the extract and then answer the questions.

[15]

Andante

Beethoven

(a) Add the correct time signature at the places marked ∗ . [2]

(b) The key is G minor. [1]

Name the other key that has the same key signature. _____

(c) Give the technical names (e.g. tonic, dominant) of the notes marked **A** and **B**. [2]

A (bar 3) _____ **B** (bar 4) _____

(d) Describe the chords marked **X**, **Y** and **Z** as I, II, IV or V. Identify the lowest note of each chord as the root (a), 3rd (b) or 5th (c). [2]

Chord **X** (bar 1) _____ [2]

Chord **Y** (bar 8) _____ [2]

Chord **Z** (bar 8) _____ [2]

(e) Rewrite the left-hand part of bar 4, using the alto clef. (Add the key signature.)

[2]

2 Describe each numbered melodic interval (e.g. major 2nd).

| 10 |

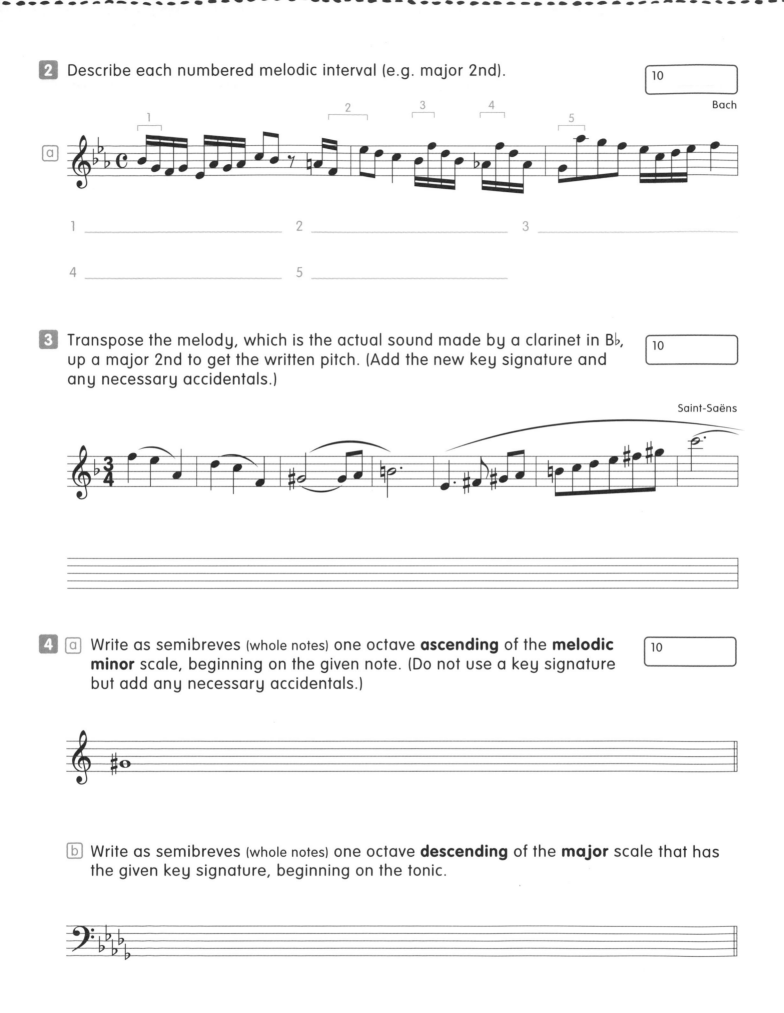

Bach

1 _____   2 _____   3 _____

4 _____   5 _____

3 Transpose the melody, which is the actual sound made by a clarinet in B♭, up a major 2nd to get the written pitch. (Add the new key signature and any necessary accidentals.)

| 10 |

Saint-Saëns

4 ⓐ Write as semibreves (whole notes) one octave **ascending** of the **melodic minor** scale, beginning on the given note. (Do not use a key signature but add any necessary accidentals.)

| 10 |

ⓑ Write as semibreves (whole notes) one octave **descending** of the **major** scale that has the given key signature, beginning on the tonic.

5 Look at the extract, which is from a piano sonata by Mozart, and then answer the questions.

Andante grazioso

Mozart

(a)(i) Give the meaning of:

10

Andante grazioso _____ [2]

▾ (bar 2) _____ [2]

sf (bar 3) _____ [2]

𝄆 and 𝄇 _____ [2]

(ii) Describe the time signature as:

simple or compound _____ [1]

duple, triple or quadruple _____ [1]

b (i) Use the appropriate letter to **mark on the music** one example of each of the following. Give the bar number of each of your answers.

10

In bars 1-4

A   in the right-hand part, a submediant of A major
(circle the notes).   Bar ____I____

B   3 successive notes that form the subdominant
triad of A major (circle the notes).   Bar _____   [2]

C   in the left-hand part, an harmonic interval of
a major 6th (circle the notes).   Bar _____   [2]

D   the tonic chord of A major in root position (Ia)
(circle the notes).   Bar _____   [2]

(ii) Rewrite the 1st left-hand chord in bar 10 at the same pitch in the tenor C clef.   [4]
(Add the clef and the key signature.)

c (i) Write as a breve (double whole-note) an enharmonic equivalent of the last right-hand note.

10

[2]

(ii) Answer TRUE or FALSE to each statement:

No brass or woodwind instruments could play the right-hand
part of bar 8 because they can usually play only 1 note at a time. _____   [2]

The shortest note value used in this extract is a semiquaver (16th note). _____   [2]

(iii) Name an instrument that could play the right-hand part of bars 1-3.
State the family to which it belongs to.

Instrument _____   Family _____   [4]

6 a EITHER
Compose an 8-bar melody for clarinet or violin, using the given opening.
(Indicate the **tempo** and other **performance directions**.)

15

Instrument: _____

OR

b Compose a melody to the words for a solo voice. (Write each syllable under the note(s).
Indicate the **tempo** and other **performance directions** as appropriate.)

Little drops of water,
Little grains of sand,
Make the mighty ocean
And the pleasant land.

Ebenezer Cobham Brewer

7 Suggest suitable progressions for the cadences by indicating ONLY ONE chord (I, II, IV or V) at each of the places marked **A-E**.

10

Show the chords:

EITHER ⓐ by writing I, II etc. on the lines;

OR ⓑ by writing notes on the staves.

First Cadence:

Chord **A** _____

Chord **B** _____

Second Cadence:

Chord **C** _____

Chord **D** _____

Chord **E** _____

If you have any comments, questions, or suggestions about this series, please feel free to email us at: poco_studio@yahoo.co.uk

Revision Notes

Tenor clef

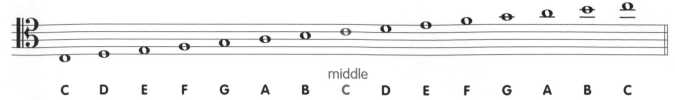

| C | D | E | F | G | A | B | middle C | D | E | F | G | A | B | C |

Notes & rests

Time name	breve (double whole note)	semibreve (whole note)	minim (half note)	crotchet (quarter note)	quaver (eighth note)	semiquaver (16th note)	demisemiquaver (32nd note)
Note							
Rest							

- breve rest = a whole bar rest in $\frac{4}{2}$
- semibreve rest = a whole bar rest in any time signature (except $\frac{4}{2}$)

Simple & compound time

	Simple time			Compound time		
Duple	$\frac{2}{2}$ 2 minim beats	$\frac{2}{4}$ 2 crotchet beats		$\frac{6}{4}$ 2 dotted minim beats	$\frac{6}{8}$ 2 dotted crotchet beats	$\frac{6}{16}$ 2 dotted quaver beats
Triple	$\frac{3}{2}$ 3 minim beats	$\frac{3}{4}$ 3 crotchet beats	$\frac{3}{8}$ 3 quaver beats	$\frac{9}{4}$ 3 dotted minim beats	$\frac{9}{8}$ 3 dotted crotchet beats	$\frac{9}{16}$ 3 dotted quaver beats
Quadruple	$\frac{4}{2}$ 4 minim beats	$\frac{4}{4}$ 4 crotchet beats	$\frac{4}{8}$ 4 quaver beats	$\frac{12}{4}$ 4 dotted minim beats	$\frac{12}{8}$ 4 dotted crotchet beats	$\frac{12}{16}$ 4 dotted quaver beats

Changing the time signature: Simple & compound

Simple	$\frac{2}{2}$	$\frac{3}{2}$	$\frac{4}{2}$	$\frac{2}{4}$	$\frac{3}{4}$	$\frac{4}{4}$	$\frac{3}{8}$	$\frac{4}{8}$
Compound	$\frac{6}{4}$	$\frac{9}{4}$	$\frac{12}{4}$	$\frac{6}{8}$	$\frac{9}{8}$	$\frac{12}{8}$	$\frac{9}{16}$	$\frac{12}{16}$

Simple	$\frac{4}{2}$ ...	$\frac{4}{4}$ ...	$\frac{4}{8}$ ...
Compound	$\frac{12}{4}$ ...	$\frac{12}{8}$ ...	$\frac{12}{16}$ ...

Irregular time signatures

Quintuple time	Septuple time
$\frac{5}{4}$ ♩ ♩ ♩ ♩ ♩ | ♩ ♩ ♩. ‖ 5 crotchet beats: 2 + 3	$\frac{7}{4}$ ♩ ♩ ♩ ♩ ♩ ♩ | ♩. ♩ ♩ ‖ 7 crotchet beats: 3 + 4
$\frac{5}{8}$ ♪♪♪♪♪ | ♪♪♪ ♪ ‖ 5 quaver beats: 3 + 2	$\frac{7}{8}$ ♪♪♪♪♪♪ | ♩ ♩. ‖ 7 quaver beats: 4 + 3

Key signatures

- Harmonic minor = raise the 7th note ascending and descending.
- Melodic minor = raise the 6th and 7th notes ascending only.

G major E minor	D major B minor	A major F# minor	E major C# minor	B major G# minor	F# major D# minor

F major D minor	B♭ major G minor	E♭ major C minor	A♭ major F minor	D♭ major B♭ minor	G♭ major E♭ minor

Technical names of notes

1st	2nd	3rd	4th	5th	6th	7th	1st
tonic	supertonic	mediant	subdominant	dominant	submediant	leading note	(tonic)

Intervals

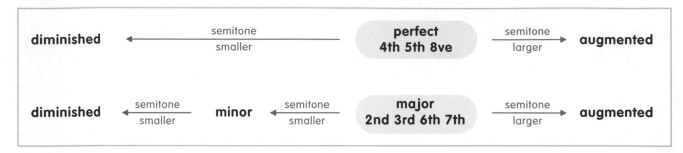

diminished ← semitone smaller → **perfect 4th 5th 8ve** ← semitone larger → **augmented**

diminished ← semitone smaller — **minor** ← semitone smaller — **major 2nd 3rd 6th 7th** — semitone larger → **augmented**

Ornaments

acciaccatura	acciaccature	appoggiatura	turn	inverted turn	upper mordent	lower mordent	trill / shake

Voices

highest ←————————————————→ lowest

soprano   mezzo-soprano   alto/contralto   tenor   baritone   bass

Instruments

	String				Woodwind				Brass			
Inst.	violin	viola	cello	double bass	flute	oboe	clarinet	bassoon	trumpet	horn	trombone	tuba
Clef	treble	alto	bass tenor	bass	treble	treble	treble	bass tenor	treble	treble	bass tenor	bass
Trans.	-	-	-	trans.	-	-	trans.	-	trans.	trans.	-	-
Other features	-	-	-	-	-	double-reed	single-reed	double-reed	-	-	using a slide	-

highest ←——→ lowest   highest ←——→ lowest   highest ←——→ lowest

Percussion

Definite pitch	timpani (kettle drums)	glockenspiel	xylophone	marimba	vibraphone	celesta	tubular bells
Indefinite pitch	side drum	bass drum	cymbals	triangle	tambourine	castanets	tam-tam (gong)